Clinical Management of Swallowing Disorders Workbook

Third Edition

Clinical Management of Swallowing Disorders Workbook

Third Edition

Thomas Murry, PhD

**PLURAL
PUBLISHING**
INC.

SAN DIEGO
OXFORD
MELBOURNE

5521 Ruffin Road
San Diego, CA 92123

e-mail: info@pluralpublishing.com
Web site: http://www.pluralpublishing.com

49 Bath Street
Abingdon, Oxfordshire OX14 1EA
United Kingdom

Typeset in 12/14 Palatino by Flanagan's Publishing Services, Inc.
Printed in the United States of America by McNaughton & Gunn

Cover image courtesy of VEM / Photo Researchers, Inc.

ISBN-13: 978-1-59756-485-4
ISBN-10: 1-59756-485-0

Contents

Preface

The Clinical Management of Swallowing Disorders Workbook, Third Edition, was designed to accompany the textbook *Clinical Management of Swallowing Disorders, Third Edition.* It broadly follows the topics in each chapter of the textbook. But, this workbook may also be used as a stand-alone study guide for the practicing clinician. For the classroom teacher, this workbook is an invaluable guide that allows the teacher to focus on important issues and the student to respond to those issues independently through the questions and study topics. Thus, students can better retain the important classroom information by answering the questions and completing the projects in the workbook.

Students are encouraged to use the workbook as a study guide prior to the classroom lectures and then complete the questions after the classroom lecture.

For those clinicians working with patients with swallowing disorders, a quick review of the question topics will be helpful to refresh memories from previous coursework.

This workbook offers the student, whether in the classroom or the clinic, another opportunity to remain current with his or her understanding of swallowing disorders.

Thomas Murry

The first edition of this workbook would not have been written were it not for the Saturday morning chats and encouragement from my good friend, Dr. Sadanand Singh. He is the one who first saw the value for workbooks to accompany textbooks and clinical reference books. The initial workbook was assembled in a few months thanks to his encouragement. This edition of the workbook accompanies *Clinical Management of Swallowing Disorders, Third Edition*. It has been expanded to be equally useful for the practicing clinician who wants to keep abreast of important issues related to swallowing and feeding.

This edition of the workbook is dedicated to Dr. Singh,
as he continues to be a motivating force in my work.

Introduction to and Epidemiology of Swallowing Disorders

If the statement is *False*, write in the correct statement under the question. This will allow you to use this workbook as a study guide.

1. _____ A normal swallow is possible even if all swallowing organs are not normal.

   _____

2. _____ Most people will occasionally aspirate some food or fluid.

   _____

3. _____ Aspiration pneumonia is the result of a pulmonary infection.

   _____

4. _____ The normal individual does not require as much water as the neurologically impaired person.

   _____

5. _____ Chewing is more difficult for people who lack adequate hydration.

   _____

6. _____ People at risk for aspiration should not take liquids.

   _____

7. _____ Malnutrition will decrease the speed of recovery in stroke patients.

   _____

8. _____ Malnutrition can be found in all patients with a neurological disease.

9. _____ Unplanned weight loss is a welcome event for overweight people who are over the age of 60.

10. _____ The study of pneumonia rates pre– and post–early intervention by Odderson, Keaton, and McKenna in 1995 suggests that the cost of an early intervention program reduces the overall cost of treating pneumonia.

11. _____ Hospitals will benefit from early intervention programs because the cost of nonoral feeding is more expensive than oral feeding.

12. _____ Adult patients undergoing surgery to the kidneys, liver, or hips may experience dysphagia after these procedures.

13. _____ The incidence of swallowing disorders in CVA patients is about 42%.

14. _____ Cortical strokes result in dysphagia more than any other type of stroke.

15. _____ Approximately 20% of stroke patients die due to aspiration pneumonia in the first year after the stroke.

16. _____ Elderly individuals over the age of approximately 80 years are likely to have dysphagia even without knowing it.

COMPLETION

17. List 2 differences between individuals with normal swallowing and those with dysphagia.

   _____

   _____

18. What are the differences between dysphagia and aphagia? Include at least 2 differences.

   _____

   _____

19. Aspiration occurs when foods or liquids _____

   _____

20. List 2 ways in which aspiration is different from aspiration pneumonia.

   _____

   _____

21. Describe silent aspiration. Does it happen in otherwise normal individuals? Why or why not?

   _____

   _____

22. List 3 contributors to dehydration.

   _____

   _____

   _____

23. List 3 reasons why dysphagia increases the severity of the primary disease or sickness of a patient.

   _____

   _____

   _____

24. Give 3 reasons for starting a swallowing intervention program early during the hospital admission of a patient following a CVA.

_____

_____

_____

25. What evidence do Wasserman and colleagues give for aggressive treatment of patients following surgery for cancer in the head or neck areas in their 2001 study?

_____

_____

26. What is the main purpose of the SWAL-QOL? When would the SWAL-QOL not be a useful tool?

_____

_____

27. Name 3 types of research studies that are needed to determine the true effectiveness of an early intervention program in dysphagia.

_____

_____

_____

28. Why does Parkinson disease lead to increasing swallowing disorders 100% of the time? Give at least 2 reasons.

_____

_____

29. Why should weight loss in an elderly person be worked up by a dysphagia specialist even when the patient has no other complaints or obvious problems?

_____

_____

30. To what did Aviv and colleagues attribute the high rate of swallowing disorders in cardiac patients in their 2005 study?

_____

_____

31. List 3 reasons for beginning a nonoral (nothing by mouth) diet for a patient with dementia.

_____

_____

_____

32. List the 4 conditions of the elderly associated with dysphagia that should be evaluated by swallowing specialists.

_____

_____

_____

_____

33. Why would a dysphagia specialist recommend against a huge insensate tissue flap in favor of a primary closure technique of a tumor site?

_____

_____

_____

34. The overall death rate from all types of pneumonia is approximately 2%. Give at least 2 reasons why the death rate is as high as 40% following readmission for pneumonia to a hospital.

_____

_____

MULTIPLE CHOICE

35. _____ Dysphagia has been shown to lead to
    A. Depression
    B. Social instability
    C. Loss of muscle bulk
    D. General decline of health
    E. All of the above

36. _____ Current research on the financial impact of dysphagia is

   A. In agreement with insurance reimbursement and guidelines
   B. Unable to determine the true estimates of dysphagia rehabilitation
   C. Adequate to predict recovery in most diseases
   D. Based on the underlying disease, not the reason for the dysphagia

37. _____ Rehabilitation of the patient with dysphagia may be limited by

   A. Medical knowledge
   B. Costs of treatment
   C. Patient's ability to respond
   D. Family support
   E. All of the above

38. _____ Of the following, which two groups of patients may not respond to treatment for their swallowing disorder? Include two answers.

   A. Parkinson disease
   B. Alzheimer disease
   C. Cancer of the tongue
   D. Huntington disease
   E. Dementia

39. _____ Nursing home residents have an increase in swallowing problems while living at the nursing home primarily because of

   A. Poor diet
   B. Lack of sufficient medical care
   C. Early discharge from the hospital after their surgery or disease
   D. Depression

40. _____ In today's society, weight loss

   A. Is desirable when people first arrive at the hospital with laryngeal cancer
   B. May have negative effects on hospitalized patients
   C. May speed up the dysphagia rehabilitation of a patient following a CVA
   D. Has little to do with the treatment of swallowing disorders in most patients

41. _____ The clinical swallowing examination

    A. Provides the clinician with the basis for deciding what type of foods to give a patient with a swallowing disorder
    B. Generally eliminates the need for other examinations if the patient is alert during the clinical examination
    C. Usually provides the clinician with a diagnosis and treatment plan
    D. May be used as a screening tool to identify patients at risk for aspiration

STUDENT PROJECT

Design a basic study to determine if an early intervention program for the treatment of a swallowing disorder in a patient following cancer of the tongue is efficacious. What assessments or measures would you consider? What outcome measures would you have for this study?

Anatomy and Function of the Swallowing Mechanism

TRUE OR FALSE

If the statement is *False*, write in the correct statement under the question. This will allow you to use this workbook as a study guide.

1. _____ There is no sensory information occurring during the oral preparatory phase of swallowing.

   _____

2. _____ The loss of the molar teeth will not affect the transfer stage of the oral preparatory phase of swallowing.

   _____

3. _____ Chewing is part of the oral phase of swallowing.

   _____

4. _____ Normal bolus movement is a combination of pressure and tongue posture.

   _____

5. _____ The teeth are the primary manipulators of the bolus during the oral phase of swallowing.

   _____

6. _____ Bolus containment is the responsibility of the tongue.

   _____

7. _____ To improve the pharyngeal phase of swallowing in the normal person, reducing the size of the bolus is the most important factor.

_____

8. _____ The pharyngeal phase of swallowing is involuntary.

_____

9. _____ All 4 phases of swallowing are amenable to treatment in a proper dysphagia management program.

_____

10. _____ Because of the overlapping of the actions during swallowing, it is not necessary for the larynx to elevate to have a normal swallow.

_____

11. _____ The vocal folds do not have to close for the swallow to occur without aspiration or penetration.

_____

12. _____ Difficulty chewing or inability to chew various textures of food is a problem in the pharyngeal phase of swallowing.

_____

13. _____ A delayed cough or cough after the swallow is usually a sign of a pharyngeal phase swallow problem.

_____

14. _____ When food or liquid penetrate to the level of the vocal folds, the voice quality is most likely to change.

_____

15. _____ Despite modification of food textures or bolus size, a pharyngeal phase swallowing problem is unlikely to improve.

_____

16. _____ None of the major sphincters in the swallowing mechanism are likely to lead to a swallowing problem.

_____

17. _____ Cricopharyngeal sphincter relaxation in a normal individual usually coincides with the onset of the oral pharyngeal phase of swallowing.

_____

18. _____ Failure of the velopharyngeal sphincter to close during a swallow is most likely to result in air or bolus leakage into the airway.

_____

19. _____ The most important sphincter for preventing the entrance of food or liquid into the subglottic airway is the vocal folds.

_____

20. _____ The upper esophageal sphincter is normally in a state of tonic contraction when the patient is not swallowing.

_____

21. _____ The internal branch of the superior nerve is responsible for glottic closure during the passage of the bolus to the esophagus.

_____

22. _____ The superior laryngeal nerve has both sensory and motor functions.

_____

23. _____ Cortical regulation of swallowing is represented in the LEFT hemisphere of the brain.

_____

24. _____ The central pattern generator for coordinating the act of swallowing is located in the brainstem.

_____

25. _____ The voluntary and involuntary phases of swallowing are partially ongoing in the same time frame when swallowing is normal.

_____

MULTIPLE CHOICE

26. _____ Which of the following is not a part of the pharyngeal phase of swallowing

   A. Laryngeal elevation
   B. Gastroesophageal reflux
   C. Multiple swallows of one bolus
   D. Penetration of bolus to the level of the false vocal folds

27. _____ The esophagus extends from the

   A. Base of the tongue to the cricopharyngeus muscle
   B. From the true vocal folds to the entrance to the stomach
   C. From an area just inferior to the cricopharyngeus muscle to the entrance to the stomach
   D. From the base of the nasopharynx to the entrance of the stomach

28. _____ The internal branch of the superior laryngeal nerve is responsible for input to the higher levels of swallowing from

   A. Base of tongue, larynx, and esophagus
   B. False vocal folds, true vocal folds, and cricopharyngeus muscle
   C. Esophageal body
   D. Vocal folds only

29. _____ Injury to the motor branch of the vagus nerve results in

   A. Inadequate velopharyngeal closure
   B. Inadequate vocal fold closure
   C. Possible nasal regurgitation
   D. Pooling of bolus residue in the hypopharynx
   E. All of the above

30. _____ The involuntary phases of swallowing are regulated by

   A. Unilateral cortical representation
   B. Unilateral brainstem representation
   C. Bilateral brainstem representation
   D. Sensory and motor branches of CN X

STUDENT PROJECTS

1. Label the accompanying picture. Use proper anatomy names.

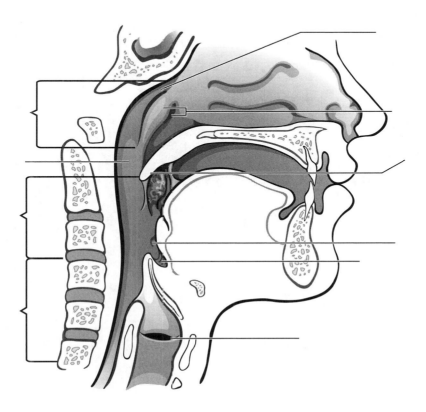

2. Design a table showing all the cranial nerves of the swallowing mechanism. Indicate whether they are sensory, motor, or both sensory and motor.

3. Draw 4 sketches that show the main structures of the swallow passageway and place the bolus in the correct location of each phase of the swallow.

1.   2.

3.   4.

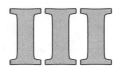

The Abnormal Swallow: Conditions and Diseases

Match the names of the cranial nerves with their cranial nerve number.

1. _____ Facial   A. CN XII

2. _____ Trigeminal   B. CN X

3. _____ Vagus   C. CN IX

4. _____ Glossopharyngeal   D. CN VII

5. _____ Hypoglossal   E. CN V

Matching

6. _____ Uncleared liquids   A. Aspiration before the swallow

7. _____ Weakness in the tongue   B. Aspiration during the swallow

8. _____ Lack of vocal fold closure C. Aspiration after the swallow

9. _____ No sensation in faucial arches

10. _____ Residue in the piriform sinuses

Matching

11. _____ ARDS   A. Bacterial infiltrates in the lungs

12. _____ Lipoid pneumonia B. Low grade fever with compromised breathing

13. _____ Aspiration pneumonia   C. Oil based fluids in the lungs

14. _____ Chronic pneumonitis   D. Lung edema

COMPLETION

Select the best answer.

15. _____ Muscles of mastication are innervated by what nerve?
    A. Glossopharyngeal
    B. Trigeminal
    C. Vagus
    D. Facial

16. _____ Muscles of the oropharynx are controlled by what nerve?
    A. CN VII
    B. CN IX
    C. CN X
    D. CN XII

17. _____ Normal swallow includes
    A. Vocal fold approximation
    B. Laryngeal elevation
    C. Stoppage of breathing
    D. Only A and C
    E. A, B, and C

18. _____ The larynx is moved anteriorly by the
    A. Relaxation of the suprahyoid muscles
    B. Contraction of the suprahyoid muscles
    C. Contraction of the vocalis muscles
    D. Relaxation of the inferior constrictor muscles

19. _____ Following the normal swallow, normal respiration begins with

    A. Normal inhalation
    B. Normal exhalation
    C. Continued breath holding
    D. Either inhalation or exhalation

20. Define the following terms.

    Prandial _____

    Preprandial _____

    Postprandial _____

21. Term that indicates that the bolus has entered the airway but has not gone below the vocal folds.

    _____

22. Swallowing event after the bolus has reached the pharyngeal phase of swallow is called:

    _____

23. Name 5 factors that are related to the acquisition of aspiration pneumonia.

    _____

    _____

    _____

    _____

24. What is the major difference between community-acquired pneumonia (CAP) and nosocomial acquired pneumonia?

    _____

    _____

    _____

25. Name the 3 distinct types of aspiration pneumonia and give an example.

    _____

    _____

    _____

26. _____ The standard test for determining the presence of fluid or bacteria in the lungs is
   A. Chest x-ray
   B. Modified barium swallow
   C. Pulmonary function study
   D. Sputum sample

27. _____ Of the 4 groups, which group is the most likely to have episodes of aspiration?
   A. Patients with oral cancer
   B. Patients after surgery for larynx cancer
   C. Patients following CVA
   D. Patients following cardiovascular event

28. _____ Neuromuscular disorders can most likely lead to aspiration despite a cognitive disorder due to
   A. Muscular weakness
   B. Taking too large of a bolus
   C. Slower than normal eating
   D. Lack of sensory function

29. _____ Tumors of the head or neck organs result in swallowing problems
   A. Shortly after surgery
   B. Shortly before and shortly after surgery
   C. Only before surgery
   D. They have swallowing problems before, shortly after, and long after surgery

30. _____ Prolonged mechanical ventilation of 2 weeks or more leads to aspiration and aspiration pneumonia primarily due to
   A. Poor breathing ability
   B. Desensate pharynx
   C. Inability to move around
   D. Muscular weakness

TRUE OR FALSE

If the statement is *False*, write in the correct statement under the question. This will allow you to use this workbook as a study guide.

31. _____ Tests of swallowing for patients with neurological disorders are usually done in conjunction with a neurosurgeon.

32. _____ Amyotrophic lateral sclerosis is a disorder of the upper and lower motor neuron systems.

33. _____ Lower motor neuron disease usually results in damage from the motor nuclei in the cerebellum.

34. _____ Approximately 20% of stroke victims die of aspiration pneumonia during the first year following their stroke.

35. _____ The risk of aspiration pneumonia in patients with strokes increases over time.

36. _____ The risk of aspiration pneumonia in patients with Parkinson disease increases over time.

37. _____ Parkinson disease patients are more likely to have less oral phase problems of swallowing than patients who have had a stroke.

38. _____ Oral, pharyngeal, laryngeal, but not esophageal problems usually lead to aspiration of foods and liquids in Parkinson patients.

39. _____ Myasthenia gravis is a disorder that reduces the muscular activating network and results in muscle fatigue.

40. _____ Inflammatory myopathies cause swallowing problems due to the fact that the muscle over acts during the act of swallowing

_____

MULTIPLE CHOICE

Neuropathologies

41. _____ The most severe swallowing problems in stroke patients are caused by strokes at the

    A. Left cerebral cortex
    B. Right cerebral cortex
    C. Hippocampus
    D. Brainstem

42. _____ Parkinson disease may lead to swallowing disorders due to

    A. Tongue weakness
    B. Cognitive disorders
    C. Impulsive feeding
    D. Depression
    E. Only A and C
    F. All of the above

43. _____ For patients diagnosed with myasthenia gravis

    A. Liquids are swallowed more easily than solids
    B. Solids are swallowed more easily than liquids
    C. Patients have significant difficulties with both liquids and solids

44. _____ Patients with a swallowing disorder following a traumatic brain injury should be

    A. Assessed only after their initial recovery
    B. Assessed every 24 hours due to possible changes in function
    C. Assessed when one of the care team identifies a neurological change
    D. Not assessed due to the need to recover from injuries first

Esophageal and Other Disorders

45. _____ The first instrumental test for patients who are suspected of having a tumor in the esophagus is the

    A. FEES
    B. Modified barium swallow
    C. Barium esophagram
    D. CT scan of the brainstem

46. _____ Following surgical treatment for esophageal cancer, treatment of ongoing esophageal disorders of swallowing may require

    A. Modification of diet
    B. Dilation of the esophagus
    C. Surgical bypass of the scarred area
    D. All of the above

47. _____ The primary tool for examining the esophagus in the absence of other systemic diseases is

    A. Modified barium swallow
    B. Esophageal manometry
    C. Esophagoduodenoscopy
    D. Esophageal x-ray

48. _____ Patients with gastroesophageal reflux disease who have episodes of aspiration usually aspirate

    A. Preprandial
    B. Prandial
    C. Postprandial
    D. All of the above

49. _____ The most common cause of gastroesophageal disease (GERD) is

    A. Relaxation of the upper esophageal sphincter
    B. Excessively spicy foods in diet
    C. Rapid weight gain or rapid weight loss
    D. Transient relaxation of the lower esophageal sphincter

50. _____ A life-threatening disease of the laryngeal area that starts with edema or sore throat is

   A. Vocal fold paralysis
   B. Epiglottitis
   C. Laryngopharygeal reflux diesease (LPRD)
   D. Laryngitis

Miscellaneous Conditions

51. _____ The most common effect of over-the-counter medications that contributes to difficulty in swallowing is

   A. Choking on pills
   B. Choking on liquids
   C. Weakening of sensation
   D. Dryness in the aerodigestive tract

52. _____ One type of medication that may improve the effects of antihistamines in patients with swallowing disorders is

   A. Mucolytic agents
   B. Vitamin A
   C. Antibiotics
   D. Antireflux medications

53. _____ The late complications of radiation treatment to the head or neck area following a cancer are

   A. Swelling and inflammation
   B. Scarring and excess mucous buildup
   C. Dryness and scarring
   D. Excess mucous buildup and sensory loss

54. _____ Rheumatoid arthritis contributes to swallowing disorders due to

   A. Joint fixation
   B. Inflammation
   C. Xerostomia
   D. All of the above

55. _____ Sjögren disease is most often treated by

    A. A speech-language pathologist using various swallowing postures

    B. An immunologist using antidryness medications, including antacids

    C. An otolaryngologist using antacids and radiation therapy

    D. A neurologist using antispasmodics and antacids

Swallowing Disorders Arising From Surgical Treatments

	TRUE/FALSE

If the statement is *False*, write in the correct statement under the question. This will allow you to use this workbook as a study guide.

1. _____ Contraction of scars, the result of surgical excision, may result in dysphagia long after surgery.

_____

2. _____ Dysphagia following surgery is related to the area where the surgery was done.

_____

3. _____ High vagal lesions are common after skull base surgery.

_____

4. _____ Injury to cranial nerve XII following surgery is likely to result in loss or partial loss of sensation.

_____

5. _____ The tongue alone is capable of propelling the bolus to the anterior faucial arches.

_____

6. _____ Surgery for tumors of the soft palate is the best management technique to improve oral phase swallowing.

_____

7. _____ Laryngeal elevation is reduced when the genioglossus and glossopharyngeal muscles are involved in the surgery.

8. _____ A tracheotomy tube provides an additional mechanism to aid in laryngeal elevation.

9. _____ Zenker diverticulum is best treated with medication to control gastroesophageal reflux.

MULTIPLE CHOICE

10. _____ Surgery of the palate causes a swallowing disorder due to

    A. Reduced propulsion

    B. Regurgitation

    C. Bolus transfer

    D. All of the above

11. _____ Following skull base surgery for a neoplasm that involves a high vagal injury, the patient will experience

    A. Bilateral laryngeal anesthesia

    B. Vocal fold paralysis

    C. Contraction of the cricopharyngeus

    D. All of the above

12. _____ Injury to cranial nerve VII is likely to result in all but one of the following

    A. Drooling

    B. Chewing

    C. Vocal fold weakness

    D. Compaction of food

13. _____ Floor of the mouth surgery for oral cancer interferes primarily with what stage of swallowing?

    A. Oral preparatory
    B. Oral
    C. Laryngeal
    D. Pharyngeal

14. _____ Surgery for cancer of the tongue resulting in partial glossectomy will affect propulsion if

    A. The tip of the tongue is removed
    B. The tongue does not protrude on oral motor testing
    C. The lip seal is impaired
    D. A and C
    E. B and C

15. _____ Surgery to remove tumors on the hard palate results in

    A. Oral phase dysphagia
    B. Hypernasal speech
    C. Regurgitation
    D. A, B, and C
    E. Only A and C

16. _____ Surgery to the hypopharyngeal walls results in

    A. Partial loss of sensation in the hypopharynx
    B. Buildup of food in the hypopharynx
    C. Aspiration of liquids
    D. Aspiration of solids
    E. All of the above

17. _____ The need for a tracheostomy tube increases the likelihood of aspiration due to all except

    A. Lowered air resistance
    B. Reduced subglottic air pressure
    C. Reduced lingual elevation
    D. Loss of sense of smell

18. _____ The primary valve for preventing fluids or foods from entering the lungs is the
    A. Velopharyngeal sphincter
    B. Passy-Muir valve
    C. Vocal folds
    D. Superior pharyngeal constrictor

19. _____ The most common reason for not treating a patient with surgery for a Zenker diverticulum is
    A. Improved symptoms with antireflux medications
    B. Due to other medical problems, patient is unable to tolerate anesthesia
    C. The age of the patient
    D. The failure of the patient to lose weight

20. _____ Dysphagia after cervical spine surgery is
    A. Common in the early postoperative period
    B. Often self-limited
    C. Often due to injury to the recurrent laryngeal nerve
    D. All of the above
    E. A and B

21. _____ Dysphagia after cervical spine surgery is due to
    A. Scarring of the retrophayngeal space
    B. Edema
    C. Disruption of the pharyngeal plexus
    D. Pain
    E. All of the above

22. _____ After skull base surgery patients may suffer aspiration due to
    A. Injury to the vagus nerve
    B. Injury to the trigeminal nerve
    C. Deconditioning
    D. All of the above
    E. A and C

23. _____ Patients with a Zenker diverticulum often present
    A. Prandial aspiration
    B. Emotional lability
    C. Regurgitation
    D. Early onset of dysphagia with liquids
    E. All of the above

24. _____ Dysphagia in patients with cancer of the upper aerodigestive tract is
    A. Often present at the time of diagnosis
    B. Often intractable
    C. Corrected with the successful treatment of the cancer
    D. A and C
    E. All of the above

COMPLETION

25. The term given to lip damage resulting in difficulty placing food in the mouth and on the tongue is _____.

26. Voice changes, liquid aspiration, and piriform sinus pooling may all be attributed to injury to which cranial nerve? _____

27. A valve used to increase subglottic air pressure in patients fitted with a tracheostomy tube is called _____.

28. This valve contributes to improved swallowing in 2 ways. What are they?

    _____

    _____

29. A pouch near the cricopharyngeus muscle that collects food particles and is caused by muscle weakness is called a _____.

30. The main purpose of the tracheotomy tube is _____

    _____

Name the types of tracheostomy tubes shown and then label the parts of each of the tubes.

Deflated

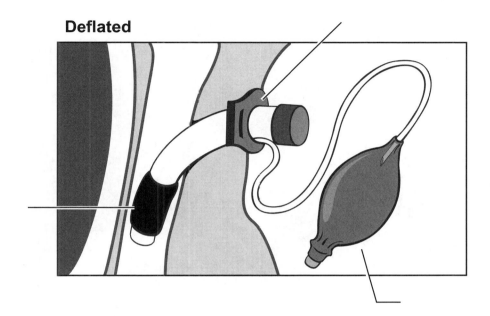

Inflated

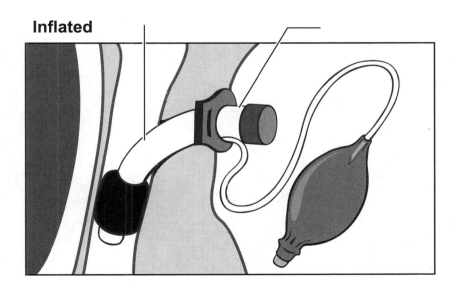

Evaluation of Dysphagia

If the statement is *False*, write in the correct statement under the question. This will allow you to use this workbook as a study guide.

1. _____ A screening test of swallowing can be done by a nurse, speech-language pathologist, or occupational therapist.

   _____

2. _____ The dye test, also known as the Evans Blue Dye Test, is a test to determine if a patient has aspiration pneumonia.

   _____

3. _____ The dye test can reliably detect small amounts of materials in the airway.

   _____

4. _____ The presence of glucose in the trachea secretions suggests the patient is aspirating.

   _____

5. _____ Ausculation of the chest provides direct evidence of penetration or aspiration.

   _____

6. _____ All swallowing patients should be given an instrumental examination before feeding.

   _____

7. _____ The bedside swallow evaluation is not predictive of the presence of aspiration.

   _____

8. _____ The Blue Dye Test is a safe and equal alternative to the videofluoroscopic examination for determining the presence of aspiration in a tracheotomized patient.

9. _____ The bedside swallow evaluation with pulse oximetry is equal to a modified barium swallow in detecting patients who are aspirating.

10. _____ The bedside swallow evaluation with pulse oximetry is sufficient to decide whether or not to start an oral diet in most patients.

11. _____ Silent aspiration is generally identifiable during a comprehensive bedside swallowing evaluation.

12. _____ The presence of facial asymmetry contributes to oral phase dysphagia.

13. _____ Normal swallowing requires the presence of a normal gag reflex.

14. _____ A trial swallow of water is not always necessary when doing a bedside swallow evaluation.

15. _____ If a trial swallow of water is to be done at the bedside swallow evaluation, the amount of water for the first swallow should be 20 ml.

16. _____ Assessment of gait during patient assessment for swallowing may be done by a speech-language pathologist.

17. _____ A thorough bedside clinical evaluation of swallowing is generally satisfactory to start rehabilitative swallow therapy.

18. _____ Laryngeal elevation can be assessed by a clinician during the bedside swallow evaluation.

19. _____ FEESST is the only reliable swallowing test of both sensory and motor functions during swallowing.

20. _____ Fluids but not food may be used during a FEES examination.

21. _____ An equivalent to sensory testing via the air pulse sensation test of FEESST is touching the epiglottis or aryepiglottic fold with the tip of a small endoscope.

22. _____ The FEES and FEESST tests can serve as a feedback tool to the patient undergoing swallowing therapy.

23. _____ The modified barium swallow test can be done with any type of foods or liquids.

24. _____ The modified barium swallow test can assess laryngeal elevation.

25. _____ The modified barium swallow test is an excellent test for the study of timing of movements of the tongue, palate, and larynx.

26. _____ Silent aspiration is usually a sign of loss of vocal fold closure ability.

27. _____ During a swallow, the upper esophageal pressure (UES) rises.

28. _____ During a swallow, the lower esophageal pressure (LES) increases from baseline.

29. _____ An esophogram test and a modified barium swallow test provide the radiologist with similar data from which to make decisions about the dysphagia.

30. _____ Trace aspiration can be identified on a modified barium swallow test.

MULTIPLE CHOICE

31. _____ Which of the following is not a part of the case history?

   A. Family history of swallowing disorders
   B. Medications and dosages
   C. Recent weight changes
   D. Evidence of trauma
   E. All are part of the case history

32. _____ The swallowing screening procedure can identify all of the following except

   A. History of pneumonia
   B. Strength of cough
   C. Safety of swallowing
   D. Evidence of fluid in lungs

33. _____ The bedside swallow evaluation does not include

   A. Examination of the pharynx
   B. Determination of aspiration
   C. Vocal fold closure
   D. A and B but includes C
   E. A, B, and C

34. _____ Which of the following is not part of the oral examination for dysphagia?

   A. Tongue elevation
   B. Tongue sensation
   C. Resonance
   D. Cough

35. _____ Which of the following is not part of the pharyngeal/laryngeal examination for dysphagia?

   A. Laryngeal elevation
   B. Soft palate evaluation
   C. Loud phonation
   D. Cough

36. _____ Two of the most common instrumental tests of swallowing are the

   A. FEES and FEESST
   B. Modified barium swallow and ultrasound tests
   C. FEES and modified barium swallow test
   D. Modified barium swallow and manometric tests

37. _____ The modified barium swallow test is a dynamic test of swallowing. That means

   A. The x-ray unit tracks the bolus from mouth to the stomach
   B. The bolus is followed with a fixed x-ray unit as it moves from the oral cavity to the esophagus
   C. The bolus is observed when it reaches the larynx.
   D. The radiologist selects the location and manner in which he/she wants to track the bolus.

38. _____ Maneuvers and postures during swallowing can be evaluated using

   A. FEES only
   B. MBS only
   C. FEES and MBS
   D. Neither FEES nor MBS, only FEESST

39. _____ The value of ultrasound testing for dysphagia consists of all but the following

   A. It can be repeated often to track changes in swallowing
   B. It provides information about the oral phase of swallowing
   C. It uses only water for testing
   D. It is not invasive

40. _____ An objective test to determine if there is paralysis in a muscle of the larynx is

   A. Laryngeal stroboscopy
   B. Laryngeal elevation
   C. FEESST
   D. Laryngeal electromyography
   E. All of the above

COMPLETION

41. When a patient describes his or her complaints of swallowing on a form, this is called a

    _____.

42. An assessment tool to determine the patient's perception of reflux is the

    _____.

43. The first issue to identify when doing a bedside swallow evaluation is to determine the

    _____.

44. The passage of food or saliva into the lungs without a cough response by the patient
    is called _____.

45. Three signs of the condition identified in Question 44 are

    _____

    _____

    _____

46. During the oral examination, the 3 features of each organ that are assessed are

    1. _____

    2. _____

    3. _____

47. The standard instrument used to examine the nasopharynx, oropharynx, larynx, and
    vocal folds is the _____.

48. A FEESST exam includes all features of the FEES exam and adds one additional fea-
    ture. What is it?

    _____

49. The FEESST test assesses sensation by delivering _____
    to the area innervated by the _____.

50. The airway protective reflex is known as the _____.

51. This reflex has a rapid response of approximately _____ msec.

52. Two fluorographic tests of swallowing function are the _____ and the _____.

53. The fluorographic test that offers a full view of the esophagus using barium is called the _____.

54. During a modified barium swallow test when barium is seen to coat the laryngeal surface of the epiglottis, the condition is described as _____.

55. Aspiration of food or fluid below the level of the vocal folds without the patient coughing is called _____.

56. A test to determine the need for esophageal myotomy is called

_____.

57. The barium esophagram is the primary test for determining the presence of a

_____.

58. The most typical instrumental test to determine the presence of gastroesophageal reflux is _____.

STUDENT PROJECT

In the spaces below, put a checkmark in the box that allows the test listed on the right side to assess that feature.

	Can detect laryngeal elevation	Assesses oral phase	Assesses pharyngeal phase	Assesses laryngeal closure	Assesses esophageal phase	Assesses esophagus function
FEES						
FEESST						
Modified barium swallow						
Esophagram						
Bedside swallow evaluation						

For each portion of the bedside swallow evaluation, enter the task needed to assess each function

Oral	Oral continence
	Tongue range of motion
	Tongue strength
	Tongue sensation
Oropharynx	Soft palate motion
	Soft palate sensation
	Vocal fold closure
Larynx	Laryngeal elevation
	Pooling of secretions

VI

Nonsurgical Treatment of Swallowing Disorders

If the statement is *False*, write in the correct statement under the question. This will allow you to use this workbook as a study guide.

1. _____ The primary reason for treating a patient with a swallowing disorder is to improve their nutritional status.

   _____

2. _____ Practicing timing movements with placing an empty cup to the lips and removing it will not improve labial function in swallowing.

   _____

3. _____ Nonsurgical treatments for swallowing disorders are for patients with strokes and neurological disorders exclusively.

   _____

4. _____ Holding a loud note for extended periods of time (8–12 sec) will help improve vocal fold closure.

   _____

5. _____ LSVT, the treatment program for Parkinson disease speech disorders, can be useful for swallowing therapy.

   _____

6. _____ Oral motor exercises should be used to increase endurance of lip seal.

   _____

7. _____ Allowing a specified time to pass in patients with a brainstem CVA is preferred to immediate treatment.

8. _____ Oral motor exercises used by Lazarus were found to be of no value in improving oropharyngeal swallowing function.

9. _____ The Shaker exercise has been shown to decrease hyolaryngeal bolus pressure.

10. _____ Swallowing cold water compared to body temperature water has been shown to increase the overall speed of swallowing.

11. _____ Rehabilitative swallow therapy uses foods and therefore does not include compensatory techniques.

12. _____ The supraglottic swallow maneuver is the best technique for achieving vocal fold closure for a swallow.

13. _____ Teaching a swallow postural technique to dysphagic patients should be done after the instrumental swallow assessment is completed.

14. _____ A head tilt strategy during swallow to the stronger side of the pharynx will direct a bolus down the weak side.

15. _____ Occasional aspiration is to be expected in patients undergoing rehabilitative swallowing therapy.

16. _____ The number of people who develop aspiration pneumonia is about the same as the number of people who aspirate with liquids or solids.

17. _____ Aspiration in a patient with a decreased medical condition or surgical condition is a risk factor for aspiration pneumonia.

   _____

18. _____ Compensatory therapy offers treatment to the oral preparatory and oral phases of swallowing only.

   _____

19. _____ Currently, there is no evidence to support the use of lingual exercises for patients with swallowing disorders.

   _____

20. _____ LSVT therapy may be useful for both swallowing and for speech improvement in patients who have Parkinson disease and other neurological disorders.

   _____

COMPLETION

21. Name the 3 nonsurgical treatment modalities for swallowing disorders.

   1. _____
   2. _____
   3. _____

22. Name 3 purposes for using swallowing postures.

   1. _____
   2. _____
   3. _____

23. When a patient has a unilateral vocal fold paralysis or surgical removal of the vocal fold, the most effective postural adjustment is the _____.

24. Name the 3 conditions in which the chin tuck (chin down) during the swallow has been shown to be efficacious on instrumental swallow studies.

   1. _____
   2. _____
   3. _____

25. One way to move the cricoid away from the posterior pharyngeal wall in order to lower the resting sphincter pressure is to _____.

26. Tongue strengthening exercises can improve at least 3 functions in the oral phase of swallowing:

    1. _____

    2. _____

    3. _____

27. Inserting wires into the muscles of swallowing to measure the electrical activity of the muscles is called _____ stimulation.

28. The 4-step maneuver that involves breath holding while swallowing and then coughing after is called the _____.

29. What swallowing technique is hypothesized to increase the opening of the UES by holding up the thyroid cartilage?

    _____

30. The majority of research that has been done on various postures for swallowing and the one that has been found to be most useful in protecting the airway has been the

    _____.

MULTIPLE CHOICE

31. _____ Changes in treatment may be affected by
    A. Treatment technique
    B. Passage of time
    C. Strength of the patient
    D. Types of food eaten
    E. Only A, B, and C
    F. A, B, C, and D

32. _____ Compensatory swallowing therapy involves all of the following except

    A. Oral strength control

    B. Changing the size of the bolus to be swallowed

    C. Stimulating lips/tongue

    D. Improving breath holding ability

33. _____ Compensatory swallowing is limited by which of the following

    A. Time since onset of dysphagia

    B. Lack of evidence that shows it is efficacious

    C. Willingness to practice independently

    D. All of the above

34. _____ The Shaker exercise was developed primarily to

    A. Increase the opening of the UES

    B. Decrease the opening of the UES

    C. Increase the opening of the LES

    D. Decrease the opening of the LES

35. _____ Thermal stimulation is an exercise to stimulate

    A. Tongue elevation

    B. Oral awareness to the brainstem

    C. Taste

    D. All of the above

36. _____ The primary member of the team in the nonsurgical management of swallowing disorders is the

    A. Neurologist

    B. Speech-language pathologist

    C. Physical therapist

    D. Otolaryngologist

37. _____ Compensatory swallowing exercises are done primarily to improve

    A. Oral phase of swallowing

    B. Oral preparatory phase

    C. Voluntary phases

    D. Pharyngeal phase

    E. Only A and B

    F. A, B, and C

38. _____ Exercises for strengthening lip and tongue may work best on patients who

A. Have minimal cognitive disorders
B. Are highly motivated
C. Have myasthenia gravis
D. A and B only
E. A, B, and C

39. _____ The use of the chin tuck to improve safe swallowing

A. Increases the speed of the bolus to the upper esophageal sphincter
B. Prevents aspiration and penetration
C. Reduces the speed of the bolus transit in the oral cavity
D. Reduces the distance between the thyroid cartilage and the hyoid bone

40. _____ The primary outcome from studies using the Shaker exercise is

A. Significant increase in the anterior excursion of the larynx
B. Reduced opening of the upper esophageal sphincter
C. Decrease in the hypopharyngeal intrabolus pressure
D. No improvement in the types of liquid that patients with UES difficulty could swallow

41. _____ In the interest of swallowing safety, who of the following should not be involved in the treatment of patients with swallowing difficulties?

A. Occupational therapist
B. Physical therapist
C. Family member
D. Clergy
E. Gastroenterologist
F. A, C, and D
G. C and D
H. C, D, and E

For each of the swallow maneuvers listed on the left-hand side of the table, give the swallowing problem for which the maneuver is used in the center column and what the successful outcome should be when done in the right-hand column.

Maneuver	Problem	Successful Outcome
Supraglottic swallow	1.	1.
	2.	2.
Super-supraglottic swallow	1.	1.
Effortful swallow	1.	1.
Mendelsohn maneuver	1.	1.
	2.	2.
Masako maneuver	1.	1.

DISCUSSION TOPICS

1. Give a rationale for using lip and tongue exercises for a patient who has a neuromuscular disease resulting in fatigue when swallowing and occasional coughing or choking at the end of the meal.

2. In counseling patients preparing for surgery for oral cancer, what kinds of information would you give them about their future abilities to speak and swallow? Assume that you do not know the extent of their surgery (which is often the case).

Prosthetic Management of Swallowing Disorders

If the statement is *False*, write in the correct statement under the question. This will allow you to use this workbook as a study guide.

1. _____ Therabite is an object to aid the patient in increasing tongue pressure.

   _____

2. _____ Oral prosthetics is the science of providing suitable substitutes for missing, lost, or removed structures in the oral cavity.

   _____

3. _____ The use of special utensils to aid in swallowing is part of the prosthetic management of swallowing disorders.

   _____

4. _____ The role of the speech-language pathologist in prosthetic management of swallowing disorders is limited primarily to observation of the prosthetic fitting.

   _____

5. _____ Following tumor resection for oral cancer, the patient can expect to have both speech and swallowing problems.

   _____

6. _____ Patients can maintain a diet adequate in calories and in weight control without the need for dentures.

   _____

7. _____ Quality of life will not change in a patient who has been on a liquid-only diet and who can now have a more normal diet with the addition of dentures.

8. _____ The palatal reshaping prosthesis is mostly used to lift the palate to allow liquids to flow more freely.

9. _____ Implanted dentures are more expensive than and not as useful as standard dentures as they will slip and move with changing age of the patient.

10. _____ Prosthetic fitting should be done at the time of surgery if possible rather than waiting until the patient begins oral feeding.

11. _____ The prosthetic device used to improve swallowing will usually also help to improve speech production.

12. _____ A properly fitted dental appliance cannot improve the speed of eating, only the types of food consistencies.

13. _____ Prosthetic management of the hard palate for swallowing usually begins 2 to 3 weeks after the surgical area has healed.

MULTIPLE CHOICE

14. _____ Following total glossectomy, patients will
   A. Only be able to swallow liquids
   B. Be able to swallow both liquids and solids
   C. Will not be able to swallow liquids but will be able to swallow soft foods
   D. Swallow only with the aid of a tongue prosthesis

15. _____ A speaking valve over the open tracheotomy provides the patient with which of the following?

   A. Increased subglottic pressure during swallowing
   B. Increased loudness of the voice
   C. Increased strength of cough
   D. Only A and B
   E. A, B, and C

16. _____ Prosthetic management of patients following head and neck surgery includes all but

   A. The reduction of thick secretions once the prosthetic device is in place
   B. Improved physical appearance
   C. Reduced reliance on nonoral feeding
   D. Increased speed of bolus transit

17. _____ Following the diagnosis of a tumor in the tongue and surgery to remove part of the tongue, the speech-language pathologist's role is to

   A. Begin tongue strengthening exercises with the residual tongue
   B. Conduct a clinical assessment of swallowing
   C. Order a modified barium swallow or FEES study
   D. Wait until the patient is discharged from the hospital to begin swallowing therapy

18. _____ The incidence of swallowing problems following oral surgery is

   A. Greater than the incidence of speech problems
   B. More severe as the size of the tumor is larger
   C. Less than the incidence of speech problems
   D. More severe following surgery to the posterior tongue compared to the anterior
   E. All of the above

COMPLETION

19. The use of properly fitting dentures will improve swallowing in at least 3 ways. List them.

    1. _____

    2. _____

    3. _____

20. The palate lowering prosthesis improves 2 phases of swallowing and 1 aspect of speech. What are they?

    1. Phase of swallowing: _____

    2. Phase of swallowing: _____

    3. Aspect of speech: _____

21. A device used to build a palatal prosthesis so that it can make contact with the tongue is called _____.

22. A soft palate prosthesis extending posterior helps to increase the sphincteric action of the _____.

23. The major effect of a tongue prosthesis when the majority of the tongue has been removed is _____.

24. Patients with a tracheostomy tube may get improved propulsion of the bolus with the addition of a _____ placed on the tracheostomy tube.

25. A head tilt to which side of the body may improve swallowing in patients with partial or total glossectomy? _____

26. Name 4 speech sounds that would be helpful to practice to improve both speech and swallowing in patients with partial glossectomy.

    _____

    _____

    _____

    _____

27. What is the best type of imaging for use by the prosthodontist when shaping the prosthesis for a patient following removal of oral structures?

    _____

28. The physical and environmental factors such as chairs and utensils that enhance swallowing in the patient who has had head and neck surgery are usually managed by the

    _____.

29. Discuss how you proceed differently between treating a patient with a swallowing problem following partial glossectomy versus a patient with a total glossectomy. How does prosthetic management affect your treatments? How do compensatory swallowing techniques differ from rehabilitative techniques in these two groups of patients?

30. What is the role of the speech-language pathologist in the decision making, fitting, and training of a patient who is going to have a hard or soft palate prosthesis following palatal surgery?

Surgical Treatment of Swallowing

If the statement is *False*, write in the correct statement under the question. This will allow you to use this workbook as a study guide.

1. _____ Surgical treatment of swallowing disorders is used to create closure techniques and opening techniques to the various sphincters of the swallowing mechanism.

   _____

2. _____ Vocal fold medialization will improve swallowing but not voice quality.

   _____

3. _____ The primary goal of vocal fold medialization is to improve the loudness of the voice.

   _____

4. _____ Vocal fold injection is risky because it involves putting the patient to sleep with general anesthesia.

   _____

5. _____ When recovery of a paralysis is expected, no injection or medialization should be done.

   _____

6. _____ Overinjection of a vocal fold with a temporary or permanent substance will likely increase the risk of aspiration early after the injection.

   _____

7. _____ Teflon is no longer an option for vocal fold injection.

_____

8. _____ One advantage of vocal fold injection over other procedures is that it does not require general anesthesia.

_____

9. _____ Medialization laryngoplasty is best done under general anesthesia.

_____

10. _____ Arytenoid adduction improves closure of the anterior vocal folds.

_____

11. _____ Arytenoid adduction with medialization laryngoplasty will improve both voice quality and swallowing.

_____

12. _____ Arytenoid adduction can change the anatomical level of the vocal fold.

_____

13. _____ Overmedialization using an implant is a temporary glottic closure problem that resolves in 1 to 2 weeks.

_____

14. _____ The purpose of arytenoid adduction is to close the anterior vocal fold gap.

_____

15. _____ Lack of sensation in the larynx is associated with postswallow aspiration.

_____

16. _____ Nonoral feeding using PEG provides safe nutrition without aspiration.

_____

17. _____ A change in the rate of breathing is normal for a patient wearing an expiratory speaking valve.

_____

18. _____ A fenestrated tracheostomy tube may be used indefinitely until the patient recovers from extensive surgery and can begin to breathe on his/her own.

_____

19. _____ Tracheotomy is a safe and effective way of preventing aspiration in a patient following lingual surgery for partial removal of the tongue

20. _____ One year after radiation therapy for an oral or lingual cancer, patients should be expected to swallow a normal diet without aspirating but with slower eating.

MULTIPLE CHOICE

21. _____ Medialization laryngoplasty has all of the following advantages over vocal fold injection except

    A. Precise location of the implant can be determined
    B. Reversal is easy even after long-term implantation
    C. It can close a posterior gap
    D. It does not lead to granulation tissue

22. _____ Medialization laryngoplasty will not improve swallowing if

    A. The medialization is too far forward
    B. Medialization is too far posterior
    C. If there is a loss of sensation in the larynx
    D. If medialization interferes with vocalization

23. _____ Surgical or neural damage to the soft palate will lead to

    A. Regurgitation
    B. Speech distortion
    C. Delayed bolus propulsion
    D. All of the above

24. _____ Tracheostomy provides which of the following

    A. Airway
    B. Ease of suctioning
    C. Improved speech
    D. Only A and B
    E. A, B, and C

25. _____ Treatment of the paralyzed vocal fold may include
    A. Voice therapy
    B. Vocal fold medialization
    C. Postural swallowing exercises
    D. Only A and B
    E. A, B, and C

26. _____ Intractable aspiration is best treated by
    A. Vocal fold medialization
    B. Tracheostomy
    C. Gastrostomy tube
    D. Laryngotracheal separation

27. _____ Respiratory obstruction may be relieved by
    A. Tracheotomy
    B. Cricothyrotomy
    C. Vocal fold medialization
    D. Only A and B
    E. A, B, and C

28 to 33. Label each of the six structures marked with a line.

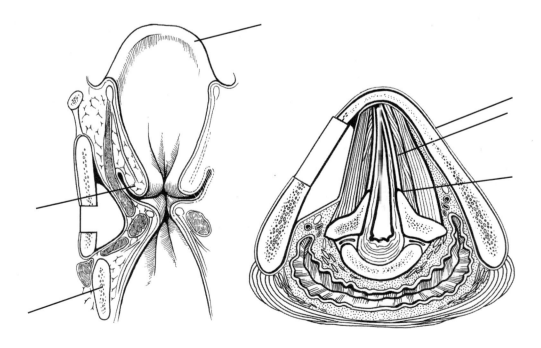

34. A growth of tissue resulting from an inflammation reaction of a foreign substance is called a _____.

35. When there is a large posterior gap after vocal fold medialization, what is the surgeon's most likely next procedure?

    _____

36. Surgery to improve upper esophageal sphincter relaxation consists of a

    _____.

37. List three factors other than a glottal gap that may be risk factors for aspiration.

    1. _____
    2. _____
    3. _____

38. A major contraindication for a cricopharyngeal myotomy is_____.

39. To improve relaxation in the area mentioned in Question 36, the best nonsurgical approach is to use the _____.

40. A surgical procedure in which a muscle is cut or trimmed to make it smaller is called a _____.

41. GERD is the common abbreviation for _____.

42. An abnormal passageway sometimes caused by surgical accident or tissue breakdown is called a _____.

43. Elevation and retraction of the soft palate is the primary responsibility of the _____ nerve.

44. A surgical procedure in which tissue is adhered to another by surgical glue or stitching is called a _____.

45. The most common reason for a tracheotomy is _____

    _____.

46. List 4 advantages of using an expiratory valve on a tracheostomy tube.

    1. _____

    2. _____

    3. _____

    4. _____

47. The most effective way to improve swallowing in a patient with a tracheostomy tube

    is _____.

48. _____ is a medical-grade substance used by otolaryngolo-
    gists to insert in patients undergoing medialization laryngoplasty.

49. The "gold standard" for treating a patient with aspiration due to glottic insufficiency

    is _____.

50. A treatment that is also used to treat patients with glottic insufficiency but may not be

    permanent is called _____.

Pediatric Swallowing and Feeding Disorders

If the statement is *False*, write in the correct statement under the question. This will allow you to use this workbook as a study guide.

1. _____ Children with low birth weight are most likely to swallow normally if they have no other neurological or muscular problems.

   _____

2. _____ Children with low birth weight are not at risk for penetration or aspiration at birth if they do not have neurological or neuromuscular disorders.

   _____

3. _____ Up to 89% of children born with cerebral palsy may have a swallowing problem.

   _____

4. _____ The pediatric feeding and swallowing team includes the parent.

   _____

5. _____ Gastroesophageal reflux is primarily an adult disorder and rarely found in children.

   _____

6. _____ In the newborn, the tongue and epiglottis are approximate to each other.

   _____

7. _____ The small oral cavity in the infant is part of the reason that children have so much difficulty swallowing at or shortly after birth.

8. _____ The respiratory and digestive pathways of humans separate by age 6 to 7 years.

9. _____ The FEES exam should be avoided in children as it is an invasive procedure and likely to cause injury to the child due to movement.

10. _____ Nonnutritive sucking may be a pacifying procedure for the child but it does not affect the ability to swallow.

11. _____ The larynx is the major organ that responds reflexively to acts of swallowing.

12. _____ The esophagoglottal closure reflex is essential in the newborn to protect against regurgitation or retrograde bolus transit.

13. _____ It is best to avoid a radiological examination of young children, as exposure to radiation involves significant risk.

14. _____ A newborn with an abnormal sucking pattern will usually have a swallowing problem.

15. _____ A child diagnosed with Down syndrome (also known as trisomy 21) will eventually develop a normal swallow sometime during his/her adult years.

16. _____ Anterior to posterior tongue motion in the newborn is called suckling.

17. _____ A child with fetal alcohol syndrome is likely to be born at low birth weight but should resolve his sucking and swallowing to reach normal feeding by one year of age.

18. _____ Children born with cerebral palsy remain undernourished despite good care even in their teenage and older years.

19. _____ Human milk has no advantage over commercial preparations for most children.

20. _____ Sucking patterns are considered efficient if they have a relatively low pressure and a long duration for each suck.

MATCHING

Match the characteristic with the disorder.

21. _____ Overly large tongue   A. Cerebral palsy

22. _____ Episodes of respiratory insufficiency   B. Fetal alcohol syndrome

23. _____ Oral motor dysfunction   C. Autism

24. _____ Multiple physical and mental disorders   D. Pierre Robin syndrome

25. _____ Behavioral feeding problems   E. Down syndrome

Match the early oral reflexes with the method of assessing

26. _____ Suck reflex   A. Stroking the infant's cheek

27. _____ Rooting reflex   B. Feel elevation of the cricoid during swallow

28. _____ Gag reflex   C. Feel pull toward the palate with finger

29. _____ Swallow reflex   D. Touching back of tongue with tongue blade

MULTIPLE CHOICE

30. _____ Epidemiological data on the incidence of feeding and swallowing problems

    A. Is well maintained by the Centers for Disease Control
    B. Lacks precision due to confusion of diseases with symptoms and terminology
    C. Lacks precision due to inability to obtain instrumental studies of children with feeding and swallowing problems
    D. Is accurate for certain disorders but not all

31. _____ The newborn anatomy is different from that of an adult because

    A. The infant larynx rests lower in the neck than that of an adult
    B. The tongue and alveolar ridge act to retain fluids more precisely without the need for dentition
    C. The tongue and epiglottis are approximate to each other
    D. The newborn epiglottis is highly flexible and serves to close the larynx during swallowing.

32. _____ Sucking motion develops in the child because

    A. The liquids and foods become more complex
    B. The development of dentition prevents suckling from continuing
    C. The oral cavity increases in size
    D. Continuing to protrude the tongue is discouraged by parents

33. _____ The reflex responsible for protecting the airway during swallowing is the

    A. Laryngeal adductor reflex
    B. Esophagoglottal reflex
    C. Pharyngoglottal reflex
    D. Gag reflex

34. _____ The early infant reflex that is assessed by placing the finger on the area of the cricoid cartilage and feeling upward movement when the child is stimulated to swallow is the

    A. Gag reflex
    B. Swallow reflex
    C. Suck reflex
    D. Rooting reflex

35. _____ The sequence for a normal swallowing event for an infant would be

    A. Breathe, suck, swallow

    B. Swallow, suck, breathe

    C. Suck, breathe, swallow

    D. Suck, swallow, breathe

COMPLETION

36. The incidence of swallowing disorders in the newborn and infant are confounded by issues relating to _____.

37. Describe the 3 glottal reflexes and what their roles are in swallowing.

    1. _____

    2. _____

    3. _____

38. For a child with cerebral palsy, 1 year of age, the MBS would be preferred to the FEES under what conditions? For the same child, when would a FEES exam be the better exam and why?

_____

_____

39. What are the 3 main presenting features of a child who is described as a failure-to-thrive child when seen at 3 months of age?

    1. _____

    2. _____

    3. _____

40. What types of modified utensils would be needed for feeding a child with

    A. Lingual weakness _____

    B. Cerebral palsy _____

    C. Autism _____

    D. Down syndrome _____

Nutrition and Diets

If the statement is *False*, write in the correct statement under the question. This will allow you to use this workbook as a study guide.

1. _____ Proper nutrition can be achieved by a combined oral and nonoral diet.

   _____

2. _____ Standardization of foods through analysis of their properties will help in reducing aspiration.

   _____

3. _____ Adding milk to foods will increase the viscosity of the food.

   _____

4. _____ Tomato juice can be used to thicken a fluid.

   _____

5. _____ Food textures vary due to taste and odor.

   _____

6. _____ The purpose of the national Dysphagia Diet is to select proper consistencies to use when doing fluoroscopic swallow studies.

   _____

7. _____ When a food substance changes as a result of chewing, we can say that its viscosity changes.

   _____

8. _____ Most foods or fluids that are eaten are non-newtonian.

_____

9. _____ As a fluid becomes more viscous, it is more easily deformed.

_____

10. _____ Nasogastric feeding tubes are usually used in patients who will be on long-term nonoral diets.

_____

11. _____ Choice of a nonoral diet via feeding tube is made based on the findings of the instrumental swallow examination.

_____

12. _____ Patients with neuromuscular disease should be placed on a feeding tube when they can no longer eat anything by mouth.

_____

13. _____ Patients who are on total parenteral nutrition eat nothing by mouth.

_____

14. _____ The largest group of patients who are at risk for dehydration are stroke patients.

_____

15. _____ Malnutrition in hospital patients has comorbidities unrelated to the underlying diagnosis.

_____

16. _____ Getting the prescribed amount of calories will allow a patient to recover from malnutrition.

_____

17. _____ The type of diet should be determined primarily by the results of the instrumental swallow study.

_____

18. _____ Elderly patients should be allowed to eat a liberal diet in order to maintain their social status and outside living activities as long as safety of swallowing is preserved in the diet.

_____

19. _____ Nonoral diets in the sick elderly should be suggested earlier rather than once malnutrition sets in.

_____

20. _____ Once a feeding tube is in place in the elderly, it is best to discontinue swallow exercises as they only make the patient more frustrated because he/she cannot eat orally.

_____

COMPLETION

21. The term given to an individual who lacks proper nutrition is called

_____.

22. The state of being fed by a feeding tube is called

_____.

23. The study of fluids and their properties is called

_____.

24. Thickeners are used in treating swallowing disorders to change what property of the liquid or food? _____

25. Calculating the rheological properties of strain and stress requires the use of what type of mathematics? _____

26. A creep test is used to determine how materials _____ when put under stress.

27. A device used to measure the resistance to flow of a material is called a

_____.

28. A fluid with no single constant value of viscosity is called a _____ fluid.

29. As fluids increase in thickness, viscosity _____.

30. Materials used to change the consistency of a liquid primarily change the

_____ of the liquid.

31. Feeding that occurs by way of entering through the intestine is called
_____ feeding.

32. Three avenues of nonoral feeding are

    1. _____

    2. _____

    3. _____

33. The most commonly placed feeding tube is called the _____
feeding tube.

34. The abbreviation, PEG, is short for _____.

35. The agency that serves to regulate the consistency, calorie count, and nutritional aspects
of dietary plans is called _____.

MULTIPLE CHOICE

36. _____ Proper nutrition
    A. Provides increased strength
    B. Builds immune status
    C. Prevents aspiration
    D. Only A and B
    E. A, B, and C

37. _____ Standardization of foods through analysis of their properties will help in all of
the following ways except
    A. Reducing aspiration during testing
    B. Improving test to test reliability
    C. Allowing a comparison of FEES and MBS results more carefully
    D. Calculating nutrition requirements.

38. _____ Examples of mechanically altered foods include
    A. Ground turkey
    B. Macaroni
    C. Baked potato
    D. Only A and B
    E. A, B, and C

39. _____ Patients with swallowing disorders should avoid all of the following except

    A. Peanuts

    B. Milk

    C. Cornbread

    D. Rice

    E. Cottage cheese

40. _____ The prime variable for studying the properties of liquids is

    A. Density

    B. Flow

    C. Viscosity

    D. Shear rate

41. _____ Viscosity represents a characteristic of a liquid that can be described more simply as

    A. Thickness

    B. Resistance to flow

    C. Degree of elasticity

    D. Type of texture

42. _____ When the patient is fed nonorally through a tube going into the intestine, this is called

    A. TPN feeding

    B. Gastrointestinal feeding

    C. PEG feeding

    D. Nasogastric feeding

43. _____ In order to maintain reliability in testing, foods are categorized into various consistencies by the group associated with the

    A. National Association of Dietitians

    B. American Association of Nutrition

    C. National Dysphagia Diet

    D. American Dietetic Association

MATCHING

44. _____ Kinematic viscosity

45. _____ Linear viscosity

46. _____ Homogeneous

47. _____ Laminar flow

A. Without turbulence

B. Compositionally similar

C. The ratio of viscosity to density

D. Fluid stress and strain are equal

48. _____ Density

49. _____ Viscosity

50. _____ Incompressible

51. _____ Isotropic

E. Unchanged by stress

F. Compactness

G. Directional uniformity

H. Resistance to flow

STUDENT PROJECT 1

From a website of your choice, design a balanced diet of 1,800 calories for two different patients—one who can be on a fully oral diet and one who must be on partial tube feeding and a puree diet. List the calories and the type of foods/liquids (protein, carbohydrate, etc.) that make up the diet.

STUDENT PROJECT 2

Design an 1,800 calorie diet for a patient with a Level 3 nutritional status. Again, list the calories and the type of foods/liquids that make up the diet.

Patients With Voice and Swallowing Disorders

If the statement is *False*, write in the correct statement under the question. This will allow you to use this workbook as a study guide.

1. _____ A fistula is an artificial device to increase pressure during swallowing.

   _____

2. _____ A fistula will reduce the propelling force during swallowing.

   _____

3. _____ Organ preservation procedures are done to return the patient to a more natural swallowing pattern.

   _____

4. _____ Organ preservation procedures for swallowing usually contribute to improving the voice and communication ability of individuals.

   _____

5. _____ The speech-language pathologist's role is to diagnose the swallowing disorder and to allow the otolaryngologist to diagnose the voice disorder when both problems are present.

   _____

6. _____ When voice and swallowing problems are present, the treatment should begin with the swallowing problem.

   _____

7. _____ Advanced Parkinson disease patients should be encouraged to have a feeding tube placed before weight loss or pneumonia occur.

8. _____ Voice and swallowing clinicians have the option to belong to only one of two special divisions within ASHA, as these 2 specialties overlap.

9. _____ Vocal function exercises may be appropriate for patients with swallowing disorders.

10. _____ When a patient with no voice complaints complains of coughing after swallowing, the best examination to do is a videostroboscopic examination.

MULTIPLE CHOICE

11. _____ An oral motor examination of the swallowing mechanism is done by a(n)
    A. Neurologist
    B. Speech-language pathologist
    C. Otolaryngologist
    D. A, B, and C
    E. Only A and C

12. _____ Of the following, which of the following is not important in developing a treatment plan for a patient with a swallowing complaint?
    A. Voice changes
    B. Singing history
    C. Chest x-ray results
    D. Pulmonary function assessment

13. _____ Observation of respiratory patterns may be useful in planning treatment for patients with
    A. Voice disorders
    B. Swallowing disorders
    C. Both A and B

14. _____ A voice and swallowing center should consist of which primary personnel?

    A. Otolaryngologist only

    B. Otolaryngologist, neurologist, and speech-language pathologist

    C. Otolaryngologist and speech-language pathologist

    D. Neurologist and speech-language pathologist

15. _____ A patient with early Parkinson disease is most likely to need

    A. Swallowing therapy

    B. Voice therapy

    C. A feeding tube

    D. Articulation therapy

16. _____ A patient with advanced Parkinson disease is most likely to need

    A. Voice therapy

    B. Swallowing therapy

    C. Nutrition consult

    D. Feeding tube

    E. B and D

    F. A, B, C, and D

17. _____ Cough and voice changes following general surgery may be due to

    A. Granuloma

    B. Pneumonia

    C. Smoking cigarettes

    D. A and B

    E. A, B, and C

18. _____ A person with cough, voice changes, and weight loss should be evaluated first by a(n)

    A. Otolaryngologist

    B. Family internist

    C. Neurologist

    D. Speech-language pathologist

19. _____ The best description of the symptoms of a Zenker diverticulum is
    A. It goes from "bad to worse"
    B. Intermittent and occasional
    C. Occasional to improved
    D. It always leads to pneumonia

20. _____ The best test to identify the presence of a Zenker diverticulum is a
    A. Modified barium swallow
    B. FEES
    C. Barium esophagram
    D. FEESST

STUDENT PROJECT 1

Prepare a list of patient assessment tools that can be used to better understand patient's complaints. These would be pencil and paper assessments such as the VHI. Tell whether they are used for voice problem assessment, swallowing problem assessment, or both.

STUDENT PROJECT 2

Prepare a treatment plan for a patient (male, 73 years old) who has had multiple strokes of a minor nature but who has been functioning close to normal in voice and swallowing (no weight loss, mild hoarseness) and in his work as an accountant. How would you go about evaluating him? Who else would you involve in his evaluation and what tests would you recommend if asked?

Answers to Questions

1. TRUE

2. TRUE

3. TRUE

4. FALSE—All individuals require 1–1½ liters of water per day, depending on their size and activity level.

5. TRUE

6. FALSE—There are many risks for aspiration, and thickened liquids may be substituted for thin liquids.

7. TRUE

8. FALSE—A neurological disease does not preclude a proper protein-calorie diet.

9. FALSE—Unplanned weight loss in the elderly is a sign of dysphagia.

10. TRUE

11. TRUE

12. TRUE

13. TRUE

14. FALSE—Brain stem strokes.

15. TRUE

16. TRUE

17. Foods may become lodged in the throat. Patients may experience regurgitation. Patients may experience slower eating than normal.

18. Dysphagia means the patient has difficulty in swallowing. Aphagia means the patient cannot swallow anything including liquids. Patients with dysphagia may be able to survive on a limited diet, whereas aphagic patients will starve if they try to eat by mouth.

19. Aspiration occurs when foods or liquids enter the airway below the level of the true vocal folds and enter the trachea and/or lungs

20. Aspiration may involve food or liquid entering the airway but the patient can cough it out. Aspiration may occur in such small amounts that it will not soil the lungs. Aspiration pneumonia occurs when enough foreign material (foods or liquids) enter the lungs to cause an infection.

21. Silent aspiration occurs when food or liquid enters the airway without the patient feeling it and therefore does not cough it out. It does not happen in a normal individual because the sensory system triggers a response to cough.

22. (1) Medications; (2) Lack of adequate water intake; and (3) Fear of choking on liquids.

23. (1) The patient cannot regain strength due to lack of eating/drinking; (2) The risk of lung infection may alter the course of a disease; and (3) The patient has more difficulty coping with the primary disease due to distraction of the swallowing problem.

24. (1) It will most likely reduce to possibility of aspiration thus allowing the patient to eat more safely; (2) The patient will not lose energy due to lack of nutrition; and (3) Reduction of pneumonia rates.

25. (1) Accuracy in reporting patient status; (2) Reduces the length of hospital stay; and (3) Weight is more likely maintained.

26. The main purpose of the SWAL-QOL is to identify the quality of life in a patient with a swallowing disorder. It may not be useful in a patient with dementia or one who has short-term memory loss.

27. (1) Studies with control groups; (2) Studies with validated outcome measures; (3) Studies with randomized treatment groups; and (4) Studies that are prospective rather than retrospective.

28. (1) There is a continuing decrease in neuromuscular control; and (2) As Parkinson disease becomes more severe, there is a decline in cognitive functioning.

29. Because unplanned weight loss in an elderly patient may be due to a swallowing disorder such as silent aspiration. Elderly patients do not usually have unplanned weight changes for no reason.

30. A large percentage of these patients had significant vagus nerve (CN X) sensory dysfunctions causing silent aspiration.

31. (1) Because they are unaware, they are likely to eat things that may cause aspiration; (2) It is important to prevent weight loss if they are suffering from other conditions as well; and (3) Swallowing rehabilitation programs are likely to be minimally or non-effective with dementia patients.

32. (1) Weight loss; (2) Avoidance of foods previously eaten; (3) Nutritional status; (4) Poor healing after injury; and (5) Increased length of meals.

33. An insensate flap may result in the patient losing sensitivity and not recognizing the presence of food or liquid in the airway. Although some sensory loss can be tolerated, one never knows how much sensory loss will lead to silent aspiration.

34. (1) The patient was sent to the nursing home before the swallowing problem was adequately treated in the hospital; and (2) There may be a delay in transferring the patient form the nursing home to the acute center.

35. E

36. B

37. E

38. B and E

39. C

40. B

41. D

CHAPTER II

1. FALSE—Sensation occurs from sensory nerves serving the oral cavity.

2. TRUE

3. FALSE—Oral preparatory stage.

4. TRUE

5. FALSE—Tongue.

6. FALSE—Lips, tongue, and cheeks.

7. FALSE—Maintaining the consistency of the bolus is the most important.

8. TRUE

9. TRUE

10. FALSE—Laryngeal elevation is a necessity for a normal swallow.

11. TRUE

12. FALSE—Oral preparatory and oral.

13. TRUE

14. TRUE

15. FALSE—It may improve with improved laryngeal elevation or stimulation with cold as well as tongue strength exercises.

16. FALSE—There is some degree of overlap to aid sphincter disorders, but the failure of the larynx to function during swallowing will lead to a swallowing disorder.

17. TRUE

18. FALSE—Likely to regurgitate into the nasopharynx or nose.

19. TRUE

20. TRUE

21. FALSE—Recurrent branch of the vagus nerve.

22. TRUE

23. FALSE—Cortical representation is in both hemispheres.

24. TRUE

25. TRUE

26. B

27. C

28. B

29. E

30. C

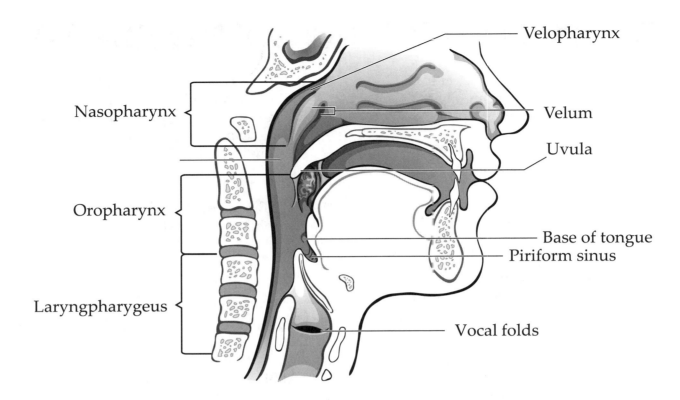

CHAPTER III

1. D	8. B	15. B
2. E	9. B	16. D
3. B	10. C	17. E
4. C	11. D	18. B
5. A	12. C	19. B
6. C	13. A	
7. A	14. B	

20. *Preprandial*—Entry of material into the airway below the true vocal folds before the swallow is triggered. *Prandial*—Entry of material into the airway below the true vocal folds during the swallow. *Postprandial*—Entry of material into the airway below the true vocal folds at a time after the swallow.

21. Penetration

22. Postprandial aspiration

23. A. Strength of cough   B. Oral hygiene
    C. Size of bolus   D. Immune function
    E. Depth of the aspiration   F. Frequency of aspiration occurrence

24. *Community-acquired pneumonia* comes from outside of the body (usually a virus) through external contacts with other people, other objects, or exposure to external infectious materials. *Nosocomial pneumonia* is usually acquired due to aspiration of oropharyngeal secretions into the trachea.

25. *Pneumonitis*—Early lung infection with low grade fever. A common problem in the elderly who claim they don't feel well a day after eating heavily. *Lung abscess*—Fluid in the lungs usually determined by x-ray examination; the person may be coughing heavily and producing a discolored sputum. *Empyema*—Fluid in the pleura of the lungs. When it gets severe enough, the pleural walls may rupture. An example is someone who is in pain and coughing heavily with productive sputum.

26. A

27. C

28. D

29. D

30. B

31. FALSE—Neurologist.

32. TRUE

33. FALSE—Spinal cord and brainstem.

34. TRUE

35. FALSE—Decreases over time.

36. TRUE

37. FALSE—They often have drooling due to muscular weakness.

38. FALSE—Parkinson patients also have esophageal problems.

39. TRUE

40. FALSE—Muscles fatigue due to weakness.

41. D

42. F

43. A

44. C

45. C

46. D

47. B

48. C

49. D

50. B

51. D

52. A

53. C

54. D

55. B

CHAPTER IV

1. TRUE

2. FALSE—Dyspahgia can occur as a result of changes in areas other than where the surgery was done.

3. FALSE—Lower cranial neuropathies are common.

4. TRUE

5. FALSE—The tongue needs a contact point, otherwise the bolus flows by gravity.

6. FALSE—Best is to fit the patient with a prosthetic device.

7. TRUE

8. FALSE—Tracheostomy tube usually causes the larynx to be lowered.

9. FALSE—Zenker diverticulum is usually treated with surgery.

10. D

11. B

12. C

13. A

14. E

15. D

16. E.

17. C

18. C

19. B

20. D

21. E

22. E

23. C

24. E

25. Microstomia

26. CN X, vagus nerve

27. Expiratory speaking valve (Passy-Muir valve is the most common one)

28. (1) Increases subglottic pressure; and (2) Restores proprioceptive cues during bolus preparation.

29. Zenker diverticulum

30. To bypass an obstruction to allow the patient to breathe.

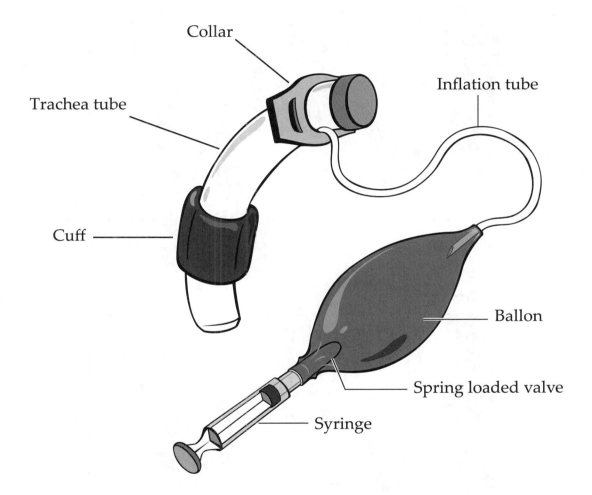

Collar

Trachea tube

Inflation tube

Cuff

Ballon

Spring loaded valve

Syringe

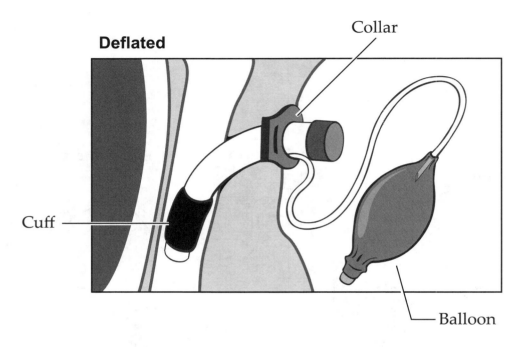

Deflated

Collar

Cuff

Balloon

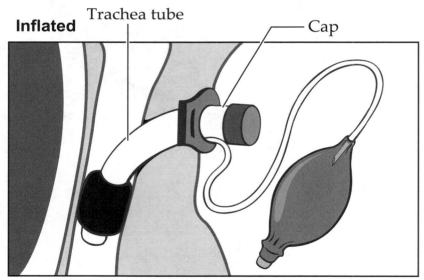

Trachea tube

Inflated

Cap

CHAPTER V

1. TRUE

2. FALSE—A test to determine if there is fluid below the tracheostomy tube.

3. FALSE—It is not reliable for small amounts of fluids or materials.

4. TRUE

5. FALSE—It is an indirect test of fluid in the lungs.

6. FALSE—Some patients are not competent either physically or cognitively to tolerate the test and may have had no reason to suspect they are at risk for aspiration.

7. TRUE

8. FALSE—It may not identify small amounts of secretions in the airway.

9. FALSE—These are both indirect ways to assess the airway and cannot directly assess aspiration.

10. FALSE—The best way to determine to start an oral diet with a test that looks at the airway during swallowing.

11. FALSE—Silent aspiration can only be determined accurately with an instrumental examination of the airway.

12. TRUE

13. FALSE—The importance of the gag reflex is not truly known.

14. TRUE

15. FALSE—5 ml.

16. TRUE

17. FALSE—Rehabilitative swallow techniques require the use of foods or liquids and silent aspiration has not been completely determined with a bedside swallow evaluation.

18. TRUE

19. TRUE

20. FALSE—FEES can use any food, liquid, or pills for the examination.

21. FALSE—This is not a reliable test of sensation.

22. TRUE

23. FALSE—All materials swallowed may be coated with barium liquid or paste.

24. TRUE

25. TRUE

26. FALSE—Usually a sign of a sensory neurological disorder.

27. False—It lowers to allow the cricopharyngeus muscle to relax and open.

28. TRUE

29. FALSE—The esophagram does not assess oral issues and the MBS does not competently assess the bolus transiting the esophagus.

30. FALSE—It may be best identified on a FEES or FEESST examination.

31. E

32. C—Silent aspiration cannot be identified during screening.

33. E—These are done during instrumental evaluations.

34. D—The cough is assessed during the pharyngeal and laryngeal assessments.

35. B—The soft palate should be evaluated during the oral examination.

36. C

37. B

38. C

39. C

40. D

41. Self-assessment

42. Reflux Symptom Index

43. Chief complaint

44. Silent aspiration

45. (1) Weak or absent cough; (2) Wet, hoarse voice quality; and (3) elevated body temperature.

46. (1) Range of motion; (2) Strength of muscles; and (3) Sensory function.

47. Flexible endoscopy

48. Sensory testing

49. Air pulse; superior laryngeal nerve

50. Laryngeal adductor reflex (LAR)

51. 0.25

52. Modified barium swallow; barium esophagram

53. Barium esophagram

54. Penetration

55. Silent aspiration

56. Esophageal manometry

57. Diverticulum called a Zenker diverticulum

58. Esophagogastroduodenoscopy (EGD)

Student Project

In the spaces below, put a checkmark in the box that allows the test listed on the right side to assess that feature.

	Can detect laryngeal elevation	Assesses oral phase	Assesses pharyngeal phase	Assesses laryngeal closure	Assesses esophageal phase	Assesses esophagus function
FEES	X		X	X	X	
FEESST	X		X	X	X	
Modified barium swallow	X	X	X		X	
Esophagram					X	X
Bedside swallow evaluation	X					

For each portion of the bedside swallow evaluation, enter the task needed to assess each function

Oral	Oral Continence	
	Tongue range of motion	lateralize, elevate, and depress tip of tongue
	Tongue strength	lift tongue against resistance of tongue blade
	Tongue sensation	light touch of tongue
Oropharynx	Soft palate motion	open mouth, observe palate movement during /a/ phonation
	Soft palate sensation	touch palate with tongue blade
	Vocal fold closure	can't be observed at bedside swallow evaluation; may be heard as loud voice
Larynx	Laryngeal elevation	feel thyroid prominence when swallowing
	Pooling of secretions	can't be observed during bedside swallow evaluation may be heard as wet hoarseness

CHAPTER VI

1. FALSE—Safety.
2. FALSE—It will help some patients.
3. FALSE—A device to improve jaw opening.
4. TRUE
5. TRUE
6. TRUE
7. FALSE—Lip seal and jaw closure exercises help.
8. FALSE—They were helpful.
9. TRUE
10. TRUE

11. FALSE—Rehabilitative and compensatory techniques can be combined.
12. FALSE—Super-supraglottic swallow.
13. FALSE—Teach it before the assessment so that it can be used during the assessment.
14. FALSE—Head tilt to the strong side will direct the bolus to the strong side.
15. TRUE
16. FALSE—Many more people aspirate than those who have aspiration pneumonia.

17. TRUE

18. FALSE—It can also help in pharyngeal stimulation.

19. FALSE—Clark and Robbins have both found these exercises to be efficacious.

20. TRUE

21. Rehabilitative, compensatory, prosthetic

22. (1) Reduce aspiration; (2) Improve transit times; and (3) Decrease residue after the swallow.

23. Chin tuck with head turned to the damaged side.

24. (1) Delay in triggering the pharyngeal swallow; (2) Reduced or absent posterior tongue base; and (3) Reduced laryngeal closure.

25. Rotate the head to one side to allow a greater esophageal opening on the other side.

26. (1) Bolus manipulation; (2) Bolus mastication; and (3) Bolus clearance.

27. Intramuscular

28. Supraglottic swallow

29. Mendelsohn maneuver

30. Chin-tuck posture

31. F

32. B

33. C

34. A

35. B

36. B

37. F

38. D

39. A

40. C

41. G

CHAPTER VII

1. FALSE—It is used to improve jaw opening.

2. FALSE—Oral prosthodontics.

3. TRUE

4. FALSE—The role is to assess swallow function before during and after the fitting of the device.

5. TRUE

6. TRUE

7. FALSE—Adding dentures will improve the quality of life.

8. FALSE—It is used to lower the palatal vault and create contact area with the tongue.

9. FALSE—Implanted dentures will stay fixed and have greater stability over time.

10. TRUE

11. TRUE

!2. FALSE—It will improve speed, types of consistency, and safety.

13. FALSE—It can begin right at the time of surgery with a temporary device.

14. A

15. E

16. A

17. B

18. E

19. Increase tongue control, allow for more flexible diet, and increase the rate of eating

20. Oral preparatory phase, oral phase, speech intelligibility

21. Obturator

22. Tongue to soft palate

23. Reduce the pooling of secretions that may lead to post swallow aspiration

24. Speaking valve or one-way speaking valve

25. Side least affected

26. /t, d, g, k/

27. CT 3-dimensional images

28. Physical or occupational therapist

CHAPTER VIII

1. TRUE

2. FALSE — It will improve voice quality also.

3. FALSE — Primary goal is to improve glottic closure.

4. FALSE — If anesthesia is used at all, it is local anesthesia.

5. FALSE — A temporary injection is a good option.

6. TRUE

7. FALSE — It can be used in patients where life may be short due to other diseases.

8. TRUE

9. FALSE — It should be done under local anesthetic to test the sound of the voice.

10. FALSE — Posterior.

11. TRUE

12. TRUE

13. FALSE — It may take longer to resolve or it may require surgery to remove the implant and replace it.

14. FALSE — Posterior.

15. TRUE

16. FALSE — Patients can aspirate.

17. FALSE — It is a warning of a breathing disorder.

18. FALSE — It may lead to bleeding, granulation tissue, or inflammation.

19. FALSE — A tracheotomy should not be expected to resolve an aspiration problem in most patients.

20. FALSE — Swallowing problems have been found to persist even 1 year after radiation therapy (see 2006 study by Dworkin).

21. B

22. C

23. D

24. D

25. E

26. D

27. D

28. to 33.

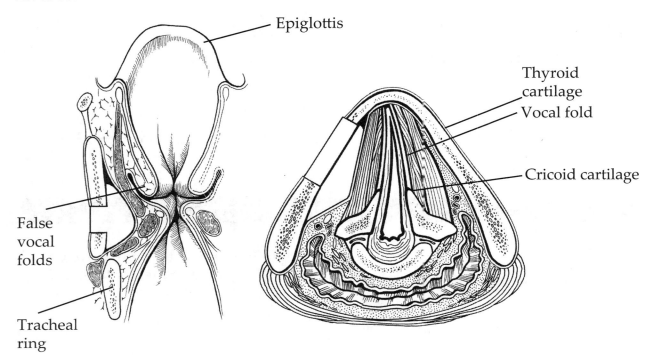

Epiglottis

Thyroid cartilage

Vocal fold

Cricoid cartilage

False vocal folds

Tracheal ring

34. Granuloma

35. Arytenoid adduction

36. Cricopharyngeal myotomy

37. (1) pharyngeal motor control;
(2) Sensory loss; and
(3) Cricopharyngeal constriction.

38. Gastroesophageal reflux disease

39. Shaker exercise

40. Myotomy

41. GERD—gastroesophageal reflux disease

42. Fistula

43. Vagus

44. Pexy procedure

45. Prolonged mechanical ventilation

46. (1) Verbal communication;
(2) Maintain air flow; (3) Increased pressure during the swallow; and
(4) Increased vocal fold adduction.

47. Decannulation, although this may not always be possible.

48. medical-grade Gore-Tex

49. Laryngeal framework surgery or medialization laryngoplasty

50. Vocal fold injection

CHAPTER IX

1. TRUE

2. FALSE—It is not always obvious if the child has a neurological problem. In addition, a child born with low birth weight may be unable to effect a normal cough or throat clear following penetration.

3. TRUE

4. TRUE

5. FALSE—Many of the gastroesophageal problems seen in infants are related to other conditions and diseases.

6. TRUE

7. FALSE—The small mouth helps to bring structures together to facilitate sucking.

8. FALSE—2 to 3 years of age.

9. FALSE—Thompson, in a 2003 study, has shown that infant FEES exams are completed about 97% of the time.

10. FALSE—Arvedson and colleagues have shown in a 2010 study that nonnutritive sucking may reduce the number of days to oral feeding in the preterm newborn.

11. TRUE

12. TRUE

13. FALSE—Although radiation has some risk, a modified barium swallow study may be the best way to determine if the child can swallow safely.

14. TRUE

15. FALSE—These children usually have issues with feeding and swallowing for most of their lives.

16. TRUE

17. FALSE—Because these children have multiple problems related to coordination, delayed development and structural defects, they may have difficulties long after the first year.

18. TRUE

19. FALSE—It helps to reduce the incidence of gastroesophageal disorders and may also reduce autoimmune disorders later in life.

20. TRUE

21. E

22. D

23. A

24. B

25. C

26. B

27. A

28. D.

29. C

30. B

31. C

32. C

33. A

34. B

35. D

36. Low birth weight, diseases, and lack of early diagnosis.

37. (1) Laryngeal adductor reflex—rapid response to closing vocal folds; (2) Esophago-glottal reflex—responds to retrograde activity in the esophagus; and (3) Pharyngoglottal reflex—responds to retrograde activity in the pharynx.

38. MBS allows one to observe oral activity; FEES allows one to observe vocal fold closure and subsequent swallows if there is pooling of secretions in the valleculae or piriform sinuses.

39. (1) Low birth weight; (2) Physical handicaps; and (3) Respiratory instability resulting in coughing or choking during feeding.

40. (A) Syringe; (B) Spoon with modified handle; (C) Color-coded spoon; and (D) Soft bottle to encourage bolus delivery.

CHAPTER X

1. TRUE

2. TRUE

3. FALSE—Decrease the viscosity.

4. FALSE—It is a thin liquid.

5. FALSE—Texture does not affect taste and odor.

6. FALSE—Its main use is to standardize diets.

7. TRUE

8. TRUE

9. FALSE—Increased viscosity reduces it ability to deform.

10. FALSE—Nasogastric tubes are for short-term use.

11. FALSE—Other factors may play a role in the choice.

12. FALSE—They should be on a feeding tube when they have the desire to maintain nutrition.

13. TRUE

14. TRUE

15. TRUE

16. FALSE—The diet must include the proper protein and calorie balance.

17. FALSE—Other factors such as dentition, living situation, and physical disabilities.

18. TRUE

19. TRUE

20. FALSE—Even with elderly patients, all attempts to encourage oral feeding should be part of the swallow treatment plan.

21. Malnourished

22. Enteral feeding

23. Rheology

24. Consistency

25. Constructive equations

26. Deform

27. Viscometer or viscosimeter

28. Non-newtonian

29. Increases

30. Viscosity

31. Enteral

32. (1) Nasenteric (nasaogastric or nasoduodenal); (2) Jejunostomy; and (3) Gastrotomy.

33. Nasogastric

34. Percutaneous endoscopic gastrostomy

35. American Dietetic Association (ADA)

36. E

37. A

38. E

39. B—Milk is 1 consistency and it can be thickened. All other products have multiple consistencies.

40. C

41. B

42. C

43. C.

44. C

45. D

46. B

47. A.

48. H

49. E

50. F

51. G

CHAPTER XI

1. FALSE—A fistula is an opening.

2. TRUE

3. FALSE—They are done to retain as many functional units as possible. Some organ preservation procedures have negative effects on swallowing.

4. FALSE—Organ preservation procedures are chosen based on the severity of the disease and the likelihood that the patient will retain some postsurgical functioning.

5. FALSE—Speech-language pathologists do not diagnose medical disorders. They assess function once a diagnosis has been made by a physician.

6. FALSE—The problem should be assessed to determine where there is greater severity. In some cases, treating the voice problem (vocal fold paralysis) will also improve the swallowing problem.

7. TRUE

8. FALSE—ASHA members can belong to as many specialty groups as they wish.

9. TRUE

10. FALSE—It would be best to do a FEESST to evaluate sensation as well as vocal fold closure.

11. D

12. B
13. C
14. C
15. B
16. F

17. D
18. B
19. A
20. C